The Aggressive Ways
of the Casual Stranger

BOOKS BY ROSMARIE WALDROP

A Dark Octave
Camp Printing
The Relaxed Abalone
Spring Is a Season and Nothing Else
Body Image (with art work by Nelson Howe)
Against Language?
The Aggressive Ways of the Casual Stranger

The Aggressive Ways
of the Casual Stranger

ROSMARIE WALDROP

RANDOM HOUSE NEW YORK

Some of these poems were first printed in *The Minnesota Review, Inscape, Open Places, Epos, The Antioch Review, Los, ppress magazine, Doones, Dark Octave* (Burning Deck, 1967), *Spring Is a Season and Nothing Else* (Perishable Press, Ltd., 1970) and *Messages* (ed. X. J. Kennedy).

ISBN: 0-394-70766-4

Library of Congress Catalog Card Number: 73-37084

Designed by Antonina Krass

Manufactured in the United States of America by Haddon Craftsmen, Scranton, Pa.

9 8 7 6 5 4 3 2

First Edition

FOR KEITH

CONTENTS

I

CONTENTS

II

III

I ∿

DEFLECTING FORCES

We try to make ourselves at home
in our lives
horses
in their stable
rubbing cheeks against security
and it takes effort
leaves our arteries dry
caked
with the cult of
all that's solid
but it takes wind
the always restless air
washes against the
PROVIDENCE HURRICANE BARRIER
to tell us rest
is a peculiar kind of movement
on the moving earth
our element's
unstable
it takes sky swept lengthwise
by gusts and squalls
cut into lines of energy
tensed
to breaking
furrows like
strata of tin and

lead
it takes whirling
widdershins towards the pole
and I'll sway like elms
their arms raised
witnesses
of terrifying visions
and scream
and scream

AND HOW DO YOU SEE
YOURSELF, MRS. WALDROP?

If I believe only what I see I'm bulging
breasts heavy belly dwarfed legs
queer
the way my shoulders
run out into nothing
but I more commonly play mirror
myself opposite my body
on an imaginary spot I fill
the nothing with the memory of a reflection
not bad everything's more beautiful
under glass lamps shine more
brightly in a room seen from the street
so this
would be o.k. except
the eye jumps back into my body
goes through the tunnels
of my skin sees
nothing inside only through it
to other sides to other surfaces
queer
the way my body
is empty in its skin

SLEEP

Pricked again by the sleep spindle

of course we all sleep I maybe
more than others
it's hard to face an empty house
besides you don't get up from
your sleeping beauty sleep the rule's
you are awakened

I stand the world with intermissions
night better than the day when it's
beginning to get light
I stow myself away
motionless
till I dissolve

only my eyes move to see
the ghosts my sleep awakens
the prince I can't be who performs
the difficult labors?
ancestral beasts floundering through
mud and rain whose names are

Walkinginmist
Comesinmist
Drizzlingrain?
or images of blood and phlegm and harm
games hobby horses sandlocked
estuaries of thirty years' forgetting?

dreams burn coldly with a freak flame
snow on my lids I say spring
is a season and nothing else
one third of me has never been born
harvest of darkness
I'm calling you

CLEANING

Yes I have a broom the box
of Spic and Span's been opened
but matter doesn't like
to be contained as women
know our wombs twitch bellies
bulge fat grows around the hips
I'm careful
make sure I miss the corners
just coax it
into a mere pretense of
clean lines reassure us
this world is ours
well
this house
even so the wood groans at night
little hunks of plaster tear free and fall
there will be a revolt the walls
will swell bulge from the seams and burst the joints
the mortar crumble and the house cave in and spread
sprawl swallow the street where asphalt melts
and ferments and all the elements ooze
back to chaos

MENSTRUATION

My appetite's for waking
chill crystals in the clouds
pebble seeds
Flaubert devoted years to
accumulation of details
worthless
next to a bare wall
I insist on living
with words
vicarious birth vicarious existence
each month my womb cries
its mouth swollen
prepares for pregnancy with spongy
warmth energy congested
red rot carried back to the earth

MORNING HAS NO HOUSE

Mornings everything is grey
as in cheap catalogues
reluctant we brush off the rim
of hairy dark you turn
to see whom you've married
I measure my impossible
expectations
gestures hang in the air
exhausted prematurely
my fear of being a kite among winds
your fear I've eaten tigers
in my dreams
but we don't tell about these things
we keep them down
in the body
you rub my arm
erasing the night evidence

INSOMNIA

How many blocks to ride
to count
uncomfortable
with nothing but myself
to hear a steady click of wheels
sand running
through my lungs
silence holds on to the grains
my retina remembers
colors
slid away with the light
two hundred blocks no promise of a station
I thread the story
of my failures how many more
blocks long
to lose the point
the small pain
of being conscious
spoils the dark
furry lap
ebbing female space

WINTER

for Frank and Helen

Already at four the moon
city grey seeps through the window
the sky so low I can't stir
my soup
days hardened
last year's loaves
I've unpacked my heavy coat
frost whistles
the smell
out of my armpits
my ears rough with
attention
the grass in my mind
uncut
stubbles through the snow
scratchy
irritating
for you
the cold is clean and clear
and a glass of whiskey
solid
like a monument

LINEAR

Bad morning
nothing connects
I've memorized my bathroom
this vitreous china guaranteed
words come
not always
nor on time is there
a radiance of exhaustion
not much sun
I rub my cold toes and look at
what do we have to do
with history
no soap collection will survive
in the abrasive future
ancestral sea ferns
then
throats ripped with greed
I can't see
anything different
personal blisters from
impersonal burns

SLAG

Spring sluggishness
replaces
winter lethargy
shaken
into consciousness
by the short
dawn I
slowly
yawn yesterday
out of my body's
cavities
reluctant stomach
all winter
I stuffed
food in my mouth
I've not
caught up swallowing
burned logs
left ash
left earth
my weight
is thick in my veins

BETWEEN

for Ingo

I'm not quite at home
on either side of the Atlantic
I'm not irritated the fish
kept me
a home makes you forget
unaware
where you are
unless you think you'd like
to be some other place
I can't think I'd like to be
some other place
places are much the same
aware
I'm nowhere
I stand securely in a liquid pane
touched on all sides

to change your country
doesn't make you
grow (a German doll
into an image of America?)
it doesn't make you change so much
you can't remember
I remember
things are much the same
so much the same the
differences are barbed
I try out living at a distance
watching from a window
immobile
not all here
or there
a creature with gills and lungs
I live in shallow water
but
when it rains
I inherit the land

OLD COUPLE

I

In the shadow
of his wife's flesh
quivers
with each freckled gesture
so much of it
in one skin
so ready to spread
into children
over chairs
soft cover over neighborhood
town
summer day
oblivious to its shadow
grey look
slow pension days

II

At seventy
he took to gardening
dug the beds
for broken springs
mocked by his wife
for fathering

III

His mouth sealed
tongue tied
why shouldn't he believe
she also threw that brick between his eyes
milk sours from her voice
hard to think now
dumb
not deaf

IV

Liked girls with vacant eyes
returning his own image
pure
hers took him in
and scattered all reflection
he looked into pure polish
drained
turned husk

V

I've made a charm against you
not herbs that harm
not onions
not honey
not the water you suspected
not meret jaw or dry bones

I've made a charm against you
now I stumble on your rugs
now I can't lift my arms I can't embrace you
now my jaws won't part for your cake
lead on my tongue can't answer you
dry eyes
in their net your bitter face

VI

The cock tied by his feet
false glare
a sunbeam in his throat
the blood runs cold
likeness

the cock is dead and mother well
old men with runny eyes
the wind
combs the thick grass
belly gone to seed

STROKE

Your leg won't
let you stand on it
you think it's out of place
somewhere
disconnected
at the ankle or the knee
everybody looks like
someone you know
this nurse or that
strange lady with
the alligator purse
this is march '66
your wife
took all your things from you
her needle's watching
you have nothing now but it's
because you're religious
lights and flashes
on the wall you see them now
also you have no elbow
in your right arm
this doesn't look like your hand
doesn't feel like it either
and it just won't

HOLD

Slow to stir
old woman
gone to water
till she breaks
white dust
runs out
not at the feet
(dirty)
a thing hard to imagine
root twisted
frayed edge
a basket is a dwelling place

REMEMBERING FATHER'S DEATH

for Dorle and Annelie

He'd always been pale
background
now in his bed as if
only his pajamas thrown there
breath losing outline
wrinkles hard to know from
the creases
in the pillow
deepened now and then as if
but beginnings only
nothing
that could grow
his face became
so absent
we hardly noticed
when it disappeared

CONFESSION TO SETTLE A CURSE

You don't
know
who I am
because
you don't know
my mother
she's always been an exemplary mother
told me so herself
there were reasons she
had to lock
everything that could be locked
there's much can be
locked
in a good German household crowded
with wardrobes dressers sideboards
bookcases cupboards chests bureaus
desks trunks caskets coffers all with lock
and key
and locked
it was lots of trouble
for her
just carry that enormous key ring
be bothered all the time
I wanted scissors stationery
my winter coat and she had to unlock
the drawer get it out and lock

all up again
me she reproached for lacking
confidence not being open
I have a mother I can tell everything
she told me so
I've
been bound
made fast
locked
by the key witch
but a small
winner
I'm not
in turn locking
a child
in my arms

OVERSHADOWED

Spidery running
a phantom child
all the dead are eager
to be remembered
the concave world where
souls smelled
and pleasure came in a net full of fish
glassy
desolate
the long German year
rolled through the calendar
with Christmas trees and painted
eggs amusements to get lost in
pick up a stone and
spit on it
were washed out of my hair

derelict toys forgotten names and
places bubble up and burst
I order and reorder ghosts of anecdotes
and hold them tight
as I descend
the spiral
flattens
into fog
and the doors I opened
have closed
behind me

imprisoned in childhood
I only pretend
to grow older

II ～

THE BEAUTIFUL DISEASE

The man
the man what
facing a soiled glove
fears death
fears power
fears monotony
but look my lord
at what
it comes
the natural curve
the incommunicable
wonder
brought to a dream head
all will change
it lives
until
all copies are destroyed
but the hysterical
hysterical who
demand a symbol that's
medicinal
the history of
a word's decay

DARK OCTAVE

for Edmond Jabès

To see darkness
the eye withdraws from light
in light
the darkness is invisible
the eye's weakness
is no weakness of the light
but the eye
away from light
is eyeless
its power is not-seeing
and this not-seeing
sees the night
do not dismiss your darkness
or you'll be left
with vision's
lesser angles
it
occupies the eye entirely

WEIGHT

The horizontal thread
falls and a figure
is deformed
yellow month
clothes and acacias change
a late apprentice
in the sun
I make a mirror
for the tarnish

GRAPHIC

All I see is what shows
in the pictures
headlines striking
but of no use
next to one a heap
broken furniture
glass
picture frames
it's too early
for the housewives to go shopping
she wanted to
buy a watch for her
the crowd paralyzed
by the camera
people look much older
decomposition
I know all about it
behind closed eyelids
wiping grease into my sweating face
choking for breath
at a certain angle in front of the
interrupting comments

CEREMONY

The silhouette of a man
confronts the mist
in order
to enter it
his gravity is
the death of me
lying in my trunk
for ten years
will I be able to bear it
awakening on a cold
fall morning
full of yellow light
dawdling
hands of the clock
when I
only I
am the spectator

NO HORIZON

I told my story
in the wrong order
innocence is lost if
you jump to conclusions
I dislike the fruit
of surrender
in spite of the aroma
of vanilla
it leaves a flat taste
the soul falls off the earth
blindness
barren
and like a tree
(in winter)
a caterpillar has formed
its chrysalis without knowing it
but he had a beautiful daughter
and the young sailor
distracted him
as the wreckage rocked
in the swell

DRY SUMMER

I turn imperfect
circles
hoping the break
in symmetry
means surprise
a cheap construction
wood and rope and wire
a bottle's weight
may set it
in motion
slow
dust rises where I go

FOR JOHN CAGE PERCHANCE

anything
like choosing shells
we take the time
walking on the beach
to do
stirs
feelings of encounter
previously unnoticed dregs
of nothingness
to let go
they're no longer
sitting at the bottom
but motes in motion
it takes a ray of sun
and looking
to see their torment
history is unavoidable
chaoses in whack
collect on mirrors
layers on layers on
inactivity
until

SINGLE VISION

Spindle legs
fattened hips
sedentary
the world makes sense
all lines converge
take their
position without
gap
concentrating cone
each
form
is the perspective
of another
till they
vanish
in the shadow trap

BLANK MOMENT

for Jocelyn

The distance from
day to day
not composition
but a place
paper with words
and with them or things
the possibility
of nothing in between
squares in old towns
left open
between whatever was built
but never empty
there are imperfections
in the paper
cobblestones change color
in the modifying air
black ink continues
black makes room
black encircles
the imperfect blank

FOR HARRIET

You say two
and two is
approximately
four
admitting that
one thing follows
another in
a narrative
a thread
a sequence
an addition
but who's to say you've got
to stop (at four)
no space between
you can't pick out
a thing all by itself
each weaves together
with the next
inside and outside
swirl
what has no reason to become
is what becomes
clear water on
where there was none
both sides of a glass wall

in drops
in threads
lines
sequences
additions
a water story
spreads
a water web

UNREADABLE ENDING

Old people in garrets
unreadable ending
but Count Wolgamot ate
without pause like a glutton until
he got up
and left
impossible to have
any quiet here
additional
advantage
so why not sit on a chair
in an empty room
and look
at the floor

LIKE HÖLDERLIN

got up early
left the house immediately
tore out grass
bits of leather in his pockets
hit fences with his handkerchief
answered yes and no
to his own questions

lies under grass
wilted flowers in his pockets
at the fence I pull my handkerchief
he liked to say no
"I'm no longer the same man"
and

"nothing is happening to me"

SALTWOMAN

Does 5th Avenue remember
its Indian trail its
snake dance its month of bright leaves
Saltwoman
looks for a town where no one
would make dirt
stirs the soup with her hand
doesn't know how the hunter
rides down his prey
but how he sprawls with a full
belly
Saltwoman stirs the soup
her needle sews
the shapeless world
Saltwoman sits on her genitals
looks at the
long legs
of American children
the city sunk in soot behind her
does it taste good
warm slag

HEAVY THE OPENING

Let's start with fracture
a smile cracks the window
take completion and throw it
that myth of in and out
what can I do without being torn
spend my days counting
the passing cars and be
awed by their ease

grain is ground
wine pressed
bread broken
lemon cut
a slice is a ticket
to celebrate the open
delirium of air

the pigment of violence
screams from my pores
net of holes
salty blades
pain is stored in the skin
and birth is bloody

III ～

AS IF WE DIDN'T
HAVE TO TALK

1

I want to stay and look at
the mess I've made
spills over
context
I'm always on the verge
of seeing it
there
on the edge
of the horizon
with doubt in the foreground
anything may
hence the troubled
periphery
the curve's lost
incomplete
incompletable
wind over the plains abandoned streets
general amnesia the vacant breath of sky
breath of sky
I might as well claim it's a
rag to
wipe my hands
but as long as we're
it doesn't matter
in spite of constant variations
what we say

2

With memory lost
surprise
could make no headway
detour blood to
cheeks
blind to your touch they
couldn't decipher
they'd feel
air altered
in the extremity of pores
the impossible opposite
of gesture

3

Afterwards
the first time lead grey sea
seems to explain
the horizon
exists and doesn't
if I could
find again the precise place
solid
under my foot
but memory
black wind from one place to another
the same oblique
emptiness as
"lived"
space
I don't know why I say all this
except
that openness
within your touch

4

You move from time to
time get up walk to the window
as if listening to
there's no sound from the
your thinking or
rhythms grow and get
lost between the surface and
whatever
else
there is
a neat pulse as if about to sound
stops
between our bodies
a large transparent page
I breathe without thinking

5

Precarious present
blood saliva urine sperm
drawn any moment
to where
our space curves
into bone

6

Body
ignores
its sense
lost in
a brief reflection
accent on
frame

7

My memory open
you're there
scenes I'd hardly been aware of
our faces touching
give way to the slaughter
of a surprised beast
my body vast
unsure territories
it would take a long
I mean images
what they mean to me gets lost
vibrations
distant heat
it would take a
long walk through mounting sand to reach them
I'm sure I've never known
anything in any
language

8

The air swollen
moisture
spiderwebs mildewed shadow
if only I could feel real drops
against my lips
spills over the edges
a woman leans out of the window as if there
were anything to see
a hundred yards off
cars race and a
jackhammer tears
not even my feet
can hear it
you're walking somewhere
towards me
and in a while we'll
as if things could be touched
teeth against tongue
as if we didn't have to
talk

9

Close up space
its rigorous uncertainty
lightning
hard profile
against
atmospheric profusion

10

Speed
transparent vibrations
spend everything I have to say
the house empty
noise
of machines from the basement
rhythm gave out
early
experience
of your presence can't explain
at any moment
as if for the last time
slant off the present

11

In order not to
disperse
I think each movement of
my hand
turns
the page
the interval has all the rights

12

A moment of bad listening
I'm on the margin
my life
paper memory
you
move among women's knees
and bursts of lips
along the quais
some of my gestures still with you
they've come unstuck
if I drank water now it would
take a long time down
to my stomach
no stone's essential weight
but
having learned to breathe

13

We walk and I say
but you've lost me in
the air seems gone it's so quiet
a look too wide to hold
lets sky run through
with mountains of water massed up moving
dispersed waves whole monuments
rise and crumble westward with
all but the message
of my eyelid
you're not there
not where
you are

14

The belly of an "a" and
vertigo
throws the words I stand on
into the white
silence charged with
all the
possible rains in the world
go on
fall back on
words always already there
the precise spot
available
as in a fog that
eyes burn
I carry your name away
from our intersection

15

Think twice before
retracing
a word
forgetting takes
place
in the contact
of skin
and paper
confusion
threadbare
the margin into
obscurity

16

Tonight a fuller air
as if some secret energy
all those windows (from the elevated metro)
people round a
silhouettes standing
my speed denies them
gesture
and
immobility
sheer disappearance
undiluted
impossible
to share
but the softness
inside my own skin overflows
as my mouth
on yours

17

The years in my face
no spectacular stories adorable
improbabilities
the road just
goes on
without asking
for approval
opaque pulsations
the quality of light not much different
in the distance
it's enough that we're
you don't have to
frenzy of moths close to
while you touch me

18

Days interminable
walks through
fragments
of conversation and warm streets
breathing
the noise
vibrates in our lungs till we
touch
time lost
in my body
pleasure turns inside out
I'm not
astonished there
could be a
balance
diffuses light
mirrors
nothing in particular

19

Nothing started yet
silence holds
my breath
waits to speak
to be able to
open
the essential detour

20

Later
walking again
northward
breaks
the surface
the eyes would touch

21

The sea you don't
question it
may have grown overnight
your eyes run over
the moving surface
out of their sockets
as if on their lids
no traces
is anything where I think
I see it
only the absence of
direction
a draft
insensible at first
pushes an opening into
the air
for once I accept not to
crowds
with tattooed daydreams
seem to move
through me
transparent
space dilated by
fear of matter

22

The way this city plays
with our bodies
so much rain the smell of wet
cement stays in the streets
out of the old shell
we're always walking in a crowd
bookstalls river iron work
on balconies
nothing has stopped over
the years (surprise)
light seems to lean against
absence of gesture
is a move
what's said is out of the game
it hangs on
but that proves nothing
like everyone we adjust
to just those questions
we choose to see
boats on the East River
barges on the Seine
garbage in the Sekonk
float on into the sky
in my dreams too we walk
along the roadless widening
angle of the light

or run
legs spider long
breath in our ears
driven by some force again
and again
to the same sentences

23

Imperceptible road
open territory
I'm amazed you follow
with nothing to hold on to or
reject
feelings don't fit in
a closed room
once they have a slant
towards distance
I'm without defense unless
echoes of a phrase you might have said
if you
accept
space disappears
the room if it's there
is
just there

24

A flexible periphery
around
a kernel
might grow
tentative traces
take body
"you"
let me touch you
believe you're here
sleeping
revolves on
its slow force
can't stop
the opening of the night

25

Air rises
blue
irresistible with distance
place to
stay
immobile
a long time
at the edge of

26

Lost
from the start
limits
a spectacle of tiredness
waiting to have
no breath
against a wall a window
the last instants

27

Again
sliding lines
this moment in the street
description of
disappears
night visible from afar
a manner of forgetting
outside the body
letters
backtrack
reliable tiredness
in search of margins
blank rhythm

28

Waiting for the storm to break
my open hand beside me
nothing to grasp
the boulevards no longer pose with
brutal perspectives
curtains of rain of dark
close in
their dignity's undone
cold
gets under my collar
trails the window pane
down to the sewers
I've forgotten what I
wanted to tell you
might as well be
glistening pavements
light chaff

29

The room's no longer
dissolves in a rhythm from
inside my eye
what we just started to talk of
water seems to rise black and insistent
boats take off
lights grow small
talk
is so difficult
two pairs of eyes
see
two different initial
questions too
disappear
as in a dream
the body
thinks against itself

30

Getting dark
I could say night
bends over the street
or lines between things
recede
give things a chance to melt
or withdraw each into
its own invisibility
could also
a child I pulled the dark over my eyes
with a little effort
turned lizard
movement through a quiet
or other things
days held together by paradigms
of English grammar
useless
now that it's night
the choice to
or

31

The succession of days
slows down
to where it seems we should
see stillness between
our usual phrases pushing
words before us
the bat inside its cry
without them
on our lids
the light would crush

32

Superimposed erasures
diverging currents swallowed
corridors halls terraces
you never know what happened
blade against
shadow
turns the limits
separate
violence
exchanges
once a tree seen through the window
a bite on the neck

33

Immobile light
accommodates
the eye
holds
the negligent curve
background
afterthought
screen
calm lack of
suddenly no more distance
only my pores perceive

34

Takes long to get up in the morning
memory of a dream
fragment of
water
and the net of future selves
(and breakfasts) I'm faithful to
ahead of behind myself
I look at you from a distance
like at a stranger
furrows
blind curves

35

The edge of the table
"life" contracts to
a tiny surface
intercepted
crumbles
gnats letters particles of dust
a summer would be
no use but for
the sun
you see with your skin
spherical silence
lines
details
energy
gravitation

36

Lids still weighted
surface from
deep liquid pleasure
unknown
in the air where I carry my head
approximations
find the mouth
blocked
turn back into desire
to be one with
the murky
a point
within the black

37

No slush across the page yet
"my" words
drop of the Allegheny when
the Ohio takes it
the mask of context evaporates
in a mild winter
the spectacle is elsewhere
I need a book to say
I love you
the curtain goes up on
your face
turns towards me on the pillow
contracts and crossfades
into your other larger
dilated pupils no longer search
across me the impersonal
meaning there's nothing
my body hides that
you don't know about

38

As if nothing had
started yet
energy of beginning pushes towards
my life ahead somewhere
interval difficult
to close no matter
how I curve
the questions I
live in are always too big
I'm not talking about
violent wind blows the mind empty
new beginnings nor our
walking towards where our horizons
for an instant
overlap but where
I could get into my story
the road catches
up with itself and I'll
be where I haven't left